The Martial Arts Training Diary
FOR KIDS!

The Martial Arts Training Diary
FOR KIDS!

by Dr. Art Brisacher

 **Turtle Press**   **Hartford**

The Martial Arts Training Diary for Kids.

Copyright © 1997 Art Brisacher. All rights reserved. Printed in the United States of America. No part of this book may be used or reproduced without written permission except in the case of brief quotations embodied in articles or reviews. For information address: Turtle Press, 401 Silas Deane Hwy., PO Box 290206, Wethersfield, CT 06129-0206.

To contact the author or order additional copies of this book:
Turtle Press
401 Silas Deane Hwy.
PO Box 290206
Wethersfield, CT 06129-0206
1-800-778-8785

Cover photo by Phil Williams
Special thanks to Millie See, Phil Williams, and Ingrid Karlsen.

ISBN 1-880336-17-0
First Edition

NOTE TO READERS

Consult a physician before undertaking this or any other exercise regimen. Neither the author nor the publisher assumes any responsibility for the use or misuse of the information contained in this book. Parents should supervise their children's martial arts activities for safety and age appropriateness.

Contents

Your Training Diary 6
Goals 19
Progress Charts 37
Forms 51
Sparring 62
Reflections 77
Important Stuff 86
Notes 87

Parents' Guide 89
Answer Key 92

Dedication

This book is dedicated to my son David. He wants to learn and tries his best. May all children be so blessed.

The Martial Arts Training Diary FOR KIDS!

Welcome to one of the best adventures you will ever have in your entire life! It is an exciting journey--it's your martial arts journey. Your friend and your companion on this journey will be a different and a very special martial arts book. This book is better than a book about famous movie stars or television actors. This book is even better than a book about your favorite sports hero. This book is like no other book you have ever seen or read. This book is about YOU and it will be written by YOU and lots of people will want to read it. The best part will come one day in the future when your son or daughter will want to read the book that you wrote when you were just a kid! When your child wants to hear about your true martial arts's adventure, you will be able to share it with them.

The best way to think about this book is think of it as your best friend--you know the kind of best friend, the kind you tell **everything**. The only difference is when you write in your martial arts training diary, you are really writing to yourself, and your diary will have a perfect memory (unlike most best friends). When something really good happens, write it in your diary and when something bad or sad happens, write that down too. Oh, and don't forget to write the funny stuff or scary things down too.

You will learn a lot in this book. You will learn a lot about your style of martial art; you will learn a little about other martial arts; and most importantly, you will learn a whole bunch about yourself. You will learn how to be the best martial artist you can be. You will learn how to work SMART and how to have fun at the same time. You will learn how to use a martial arts training diary. If you learn a great secret combination that always seems to work against bigger people then you can write it down so you won't forget it later.

Your martial arts training diary will be a place you can go to get inspired, a place where your spirits can be lifted if you are feeling down. There will be interesting stories and quotes from famous people that will help you see the best in a situation. Also, you will find the words that you have written in the past will really get you excited about what you are doing right now. A friend of mine fell off his bicycle and hurt his right leg the day before his black belt test and he was really worried that he would not be able to break the boards with his left leg. Well, he did it and with no problems. Now, whenever he is worried about something in his martial arts class (or anywhere when things go wrong) he just thinks about that black belt test and says to himself, "It's OK. I can handle it!" It is important to keep track of the things you have done and can do.

Your martial arts diary is also a very important training tool. It will help you get the most from your teachers, your classes, and your practices. There will be many valuable coaching points that will help you learn what the important things are for you to focus on and what things to think about. When it is time to start sparring in class, you get really nervous and have butterflies in your stomach. Maybe you are afraid that you might make a mistake or look bad. Well, you should talk to your instructor, spar with some friends who you are comfortable with, and most importantly, relax and have fun! If you want to get really good at sparring, you have to relax and have fun. Your instructor can help you accomplish this, and you will not have to have a perfect memory keeping everything straight because you can write it down in your diary.

Your training diary also has many puzzles, games, and fun ideas that are very entertaining. This is a book that you can pick up and read any time and any place. Also, if you feel like starting in the middle, you can. If you want to start at the end, you can do that too. If you just want to play a couple of cool games, that is your choice too! How about planning a party with all your friends where you get some martial arts movies, some drinks and snacks, and have a martial arts movie marathon. Or if you are really creative, make your own martial arts video and show that at the party.

Your martial arts training diary will be as good as you want to make it. The more photographs, drawings, and taped interviews you have, the better it will become. You need to record how you feel before your first official class, and maybe get someone to take a picture the first time you put your uniform on. Then, it will be important to record how you feel when you win your first trophy or tournament, and maybe even a photograph the day you finally earn your black belt. All these events are extremely important, from your first day in class to your black belt presentation and every day and event in between.

Training diaries have been used for years and years. Olympic athletes, weight lifters, body builders, swimmers, runners, almost every kind of athlete has used them. It is a place to keep track of what's working and what's not. It's a place to keep track of the best day you ever had and the worst day; you write it all down. Now is the time for you to take advantage of this great training tool.

Here are brief descriptions of the following chapters:

Goals How Dreams Come True.

This chapter makes you think about what you want to be, what you want to have, and what you want to accomplish. When you are on your martial arts journey, there are many wonderful and exciting things to experience and do, but you have to decide what **you** want to do. Remember this is **your** journey, not someone else's! You decide where to go by setting goals; then, you have to make a plan on how you are going to accomplish your goals. Learning how to set your own goals and how to accomplish them is very important in the martial arts, but it is even more important in everything else you do in life. The best part about setting goals and trying to accomplish them is if you succeed, you get smarter and better at it, and if you fail, you still get smarter and better at it.

Progress Charts

A lot of people think that some people are good at math and some people are good at sports and some people are good at music and so on. It's like magic, if you are lucky maybe you will be good at something too. Well, they're wrong! You will be good at the things you work at and invest your time in. Did you know Michael Jordan did not make his high school basketball team when he first tried out for it? You could say he was not good at basketball, but he worked at it and he got better, and he kept working at it and he kept getting better!

This chapter will help you measure how much better you are getting at the things you have chosen to work at. If you want to run faster, kick higher, jump higher, kick stronger, be better at sparring, be in more tournaments, get bigger muscles, get more flexible, you decide and this chapter will help you measure it.

Forms

Forms are great. They are the best exercise idea in the last 1,000 years. How else could you practice hitting, kicking, punching, and blocking someone with all your might and no one gets hurt--not you, and not your opponent. No one even gets mad. Yet, you can practice how you would react to bad guys trying to attack you, and you can use full force and practice being instantly ready.

This chapter will help you become better organized and it will help you learn your forms faster. It will help you because it will give you a place to write down the important things your instructors tell you, and it will give you a place to write the questions you have when you are practicing by yourself.

Sparring

Sparring is where all your hard work comes together. If you have been working really hard in your basic exercises, your forms, and other drills, you can't help but get better at sparring!

This chapter is neat because you can write down the special (and maybe secret) techniques that work for you. And if some things are not working very well, you can make a note in this chapter to fix them by asking someone to help you, your helper could be a senior belt or maybe your instructor. The best part is when you start taking notes on your opponents. As you figure out ways to stop their strong points and ways to take advantage of their weak points, you will hear them say, "Are you doing something different? You seem to be getting a lot better?"

Reflections

You know in school when you have class discussions, you have them because it is a good way to learn and get smarter. Also, if you are feeling worried or upset, it feels better when you can talk to someone about your problem. This is because thinking about things is good, and thinking through things can help solve problems and make good times extra special.

In this chapter what you think and what you feel are the two most important things. In fact, when you are working in this chapter, nothing in the world is more important! When you write in this chapter, you can write about anything because you are the boss. No matter what you write about, no matter how you write it, it is impossible to make a mistake. You can be a brand new white belt or you can be an advanced black belt. It doesn't matter because you are already an expert at this chapter.

Notes

As you get older and you are doing more things, it gets harder to keep everything straight. You really can not remember everything you are supposed to do or everything you might need. What is the solution? Write it down. Instead of trying to have a perfect memory, just write what you need to know down.

This chapter will give you a place to keep all your important information. Anything that you think is important goes in this chapter, and anything that does not seem to fit in any of the other chapters can also go in this chapter.

Additional Information is included in chapters 1-6. There are inspirational stories, suggested treasure page activities, and there are puzzles, games and many activities that you can do with your friends.

Inspirational Items

Many great men and women have accomplished wonderful things. It is important for us to listen to what they have to say to us. It is like listening to pioneers in the old days. When the first adventurers went out to sea or out west or even now out to outer space, it was and is important for everyone to listen to what they had to say when they returned because their lives could depend on the new information. The pioneers can tell us what to watch out for, what is good or bad, or what's important. We can learn from their mistakes as well as their accomplishments. They are just regular people who have accomplished great things. Well, we are people who also want to do great and important things too. We can let the words of others inspire us on our martial arts adventure.

Treasure Activities

These activities are things you will enjoy when you do them and treasure when you look back at them. It might be a photograph of you taken the first day of class, or maybe an interview before you go to take your first belt test. A parent or friend could ask questions just like they do on TV. How are you feeling, champ? What's your game plan? What are the main things you plan on doing out there today? Then you can do the same kinds of things after events are over. Most people have rather short answers at the start and then they get really talkative after the event is over. These activities are put in this book just as reminders for you to notice them when they happen and to record them for the future when they will become true treasures.

Puzzles and Games

Games and puzzles are included in each chapter. They are designed at different levels of difficulty. Some will seem hard and others will seem easy. If one seems hard, then make it more fun by getting friends or family to help you with it. These games and puzzles are designed to teach you about different martial arts, different martial arts terms, and lots of other interesting martial arts facts.

Fasten your seat belts because your martial arts adventure is about to begin!

Terry Fox
Young Canadian Athlete

He set a goal to run across Canada, but he failed - - or did he?.

Terry Fox was an outstanding high school athlete until 1977, then Terry had his right leg amputated above the knee because he had bone cancer. While he was in the cancer ward being treated he saw many people of all ages suffering greatly. He became inspired and decided to do something to help. His plan was to run across Canada (5,300 miles). He set this goal for two reasons: 1) He wanted to help raise money for the Canadian Cancer Society and 2) He wanted to show that being handicapped doesn't mean you still can't accomplish great things.

Here's what he had to say: **I want to show people that just because they're disabled, it's not the end**. Terry Fox trained for fifteen months before he started his run. Once he started he ran through intense heat, rain, and snow. He ran about 26 miles each day for 143 days until doctors found that the cancer had spread to his lungs and he had to stop.

Some people might look at Terry Fox and think that he failed to accomplish his goal to run across Canada, and he did fail to do that. However, he did run 3,339 miles and he raised $25 million for cancer research. Two magnificent successes by anybody's standard.

When you set an *important* goal and work hard to achieve it, you will find even in failure you will have many successes.

Treasure Page
At The Beginning!

A treasure page is designed to capture a moment in time during your martial arts adventure. You will want to show how you look (photo, or self portrait), what you think, and how you feel about different things.

Later on you might be asked the same or similar questions. Don't worry, it's not a mistake. Additionally, in the back of this book you will find that some of the treasure pages are repeated with 3 month, 6 month, and 1 year versions. It important to think about some of the same things because as you grow and learn more about your martial art (and learn more about yourself), you will see some of your answers change a lot!

Here's what to do:

1. Have someone take a photo of you when you start your martial arts training. If you have been doing it for a while and you are not a beginner, then take a photo to show how you look when you started keeping your martial arts diary.

2. If you do not have a photo, then draw a picture of how you think you look doing your martial art. If you don't think you can draw well enough then make it a fun picture like a cartoon. Put the date on it.

3. Put the picture or photo on the top of the next page.

4. Now, answer the questions on the next page, below your photo or picture.

* Why are you doing a martial art?

* What do you expect to learn from your martial arts training?

* How do you think martial arts training will change you?

* How long do you expect to do this martial art?

GAME PAGE:
Martial Arts Simon Says

Martial Arts Simon Says is played just like regular Simon Says except when you are the leader (Simon), you are only allowed to select martial arts moves for the others to do. These moves can be kicks, punches, blocks, anything you might do in your martial arts class, and you may create exciting new combinations of these moves.

Also, keep in mind that this will be good practice for you and your friends who are involved with a martial art, but your friends who are not involved with a martial art will also have a wonderful time.

Simon Says, as you might remember, is a game played by two or more people. One person is the leader and all the others follow the leader's commands. The trick of the game is the followers are not allowed to move unless the leader says, "Simon says," first. If a follower moves without hearing Simon says first then they are out of the game. The last follower left in the game is the winner. Sometimes people let the winner become the new leader for the next game.

GAME PAGE: Quotes!

What did the author say?

Our greatest glory is not in never falling, but in rising every time we fall. -*Confucius*

What do **you** think (in your own words) Confucius meant?

_____

_____

_____

_____

How do **you** think this is important to you in your daily life?

_____

_____

_____

_____

Goals
How Dreams Come True

I want to be a millionaire! I want to be a movie star! I want to play pro football! Let's go to Disney World! We want to go to the movies! I want to have a friend sleep over! I want to get all A's this marking period! I want to get my yellow belt! You have probably had a friend say one or more of these statements, or maybe you have said something similar. These statements can be examples of dreams and they can be examples of goals.

Muhammad Ali, who many consider the greatest heavyweight boxing champ of all time, used to dream and set goals. When he was a little boy, he fell in love with a red bicycle, and he made it his goal to get that used red bicycle. So he worked hard at a couple of jobs, including one at a grocery store, and finally he saved up enough money and bought that used bike. He was very happy and he had accomplished his goal of getting the bike. Later one day, when he was working at the grocery store, he went outside to find that his bike was stolen. He spent the whole summer looking all over the city for that bicycle.

Muhammad Ali set many goals in his life and he accomplished many of those goals that he set for himself. However, he never did find that bicycle, but he did go to the Olympics, he did win a gold medal, and he did become one of the greatest heavyweight champions the world has ever seen. Muhammad Ali failed to find his red bicycle but he used his failure in the wisest way possible. Every time he was fighting in the boxing ring and things got really tough for him and maybe he even felt like giving up, he would stop and think to himself as he looked at his opponent across the ring: **"That's the guy who stole my bike!"** Needless to say, he would come out fighting!

Do you have dreams? Are there things you want to be, or things you want to have, or places you want to go? Well, if dreaming is all you want then you can dream all day, but if you want your dreams to actually come true, then you better start setting goals and making plans on how to accomplish them. This is one of the most powerful skills you will ever learn. It is like having a genie in a magic bottle who is willing to grant your wishes, only it's better! When the genie grants your wishes, you get what you want but the genie keeps the power. Setting your own goals and accomplishing them is much better because you get what you want and you get to keep the POWER! So, the next time something important comes along and you want it, you will not have to go ask some genie if you have any wishes left. You just decide if you really want it, make a plan to work for it, and then just go after it!

There basically are two types of goals. One type of goal is the really big exciting kind. It might be making the varsity team at the high school, or being selected for all-county band, or getting your brown belt or black belt in your particular style of martial art. These goals might take months or years to accomplish so these goals are called **long-term goals**. (Just think long-time goals!)

The second type of goal is goals that you need to do everyday or every week in order to accomplish the bigger long-term goals. For example, if you have the long-term goal of getting your black belt, then one of your daily or weekly goals would have to be to attend your classes regularly and to practice regularly. These smaller but very important goals are called **short-term goals**. (Just think short-time goals!) It is safe to say no long-term goal is ever accomplished without a bunch of short-term goals being successfully accomplished on the way.

Now, before we get into other important points about goals, here is a secret you must know in order to be successful. **No matter how wonderful your goal is, no matter how stupendous your plan of action is, something will go wrong!** Does it mean you should forget your goal because it is impossible? Absolutely not! When things go wrong, this is where the action is; this is where you grow and get better. You could say the more things go wrong, the better you will become at fixing things and at improvising new, improved strategies. Just remember, as far as being a person who sets goals and accomplishes them, **fixing what's wrong is how you get strong!**

There are two important points when you set a goal. The first point is you should **clearly state your goal**. That is to say, you should write the goal in a way that anyone else could read it and understand it. This is not to say that you will have to let people read your personal goals. This means that you write it in words anyone could understand, so that when a few months go by and maybe you have forgotten about that particular goal, you can read your goal and you will know exactly what you meant when you first wrote it.

The second point is you should **write your goal in measurable terms**. This sounds hard but it is easy. Just write your goal clearly, and it will be easy to see whether you have or haven't accomplished it. For example, if my goal is "I want to get stronger" it would be hard to definitely say I am stronger or I am not. If my goal was to get stronger (because I can only do 2 push-ups) and I wrote my goal as "I want to be able to do 10 push-ups" then when the day came to check to see if I have accomplished my goal, it would be easy to say yes or no. If I could do 12 push-ups, then I know yes, I have accomplished my goal. If I can only do 8 push-ups, then I know I am close.

Here are a few more coaching points about setting goals:

* **Be realistic.** In school, if you usually have a lot of F's on your report card, then do not make your first goal all A's. Maybe you should try for all passing grades, then all A's and B's, and then maybe all A's. In the martial arts, if you have never broken a board, then setting the goal of breaking five is unrealistic. Set a goal of breaking one, then two, and so on.

* **Set a deadline.** If your goal is "to learn your next form from start to finish" then it is a good goal except for one question: "When are you going to jump into action?" Next week, next month, next year, or next when? Now, let's say you want to be ready for the next belt test which comes in May. So, if you say, "I want to learn my form by April 1st!" Then you have a deadline, and you know when you have to be halfway through, or if you are a little behind schedule you could get someone to help you. Having a date and a deadline helps you make your daily training decisions.

* **Don't be afraid to aim high.** The best kind of goal to have is one you can really get excited about. Even on those days when you are feeling tired or bored or you just do not want to be practicing, you just think about your goal. It will make you forget about being lazy. Also, remember you can aim high and still be realistic. You can do both!

* **To be successful at the big goals you must be successful with the little steps (short-term goals).** The successful people in sports, school, careers, in anything, all have one talent in common: They all know how to make themselves feel really good when they are doing the extremely necessary little steps. For example, if you want your side kick to get stronger, strong enough to break two boards, then the best plan might be to side kick the bag 30 times every practice for three months. Then, when you do your plan at a practice and kick that bag 30 times, you should pat yourself on the back just like you would do when you finally break those boards because every kick is bringing you one step closer to your goal.

A goal is a dream that YOU make come true one very important little step at a time.

Wilma Rudolph
1st American Woman to Win 3 Gold Medals in Track

Wilma Rudolph was born in Tennessee. She had double pneumonia when she was four, then scarlet fever, and finally polio. She was unable to walk properly until she was 11 years old. Many experts did not believe she would ever be able to walk. They all were shocked when she was able to start running and run she did!

She competed in her first Olympics when she was only 16 (in 1956) and she won the bronze medal. In 1960 in Rome she competed in her second Olympics and won gold medals in 100 meter, 200 meter, and the 400 meter relay. She was the first American women to ever win three gold medals in track and field. A feat she accomplished while suffering with a sprained ankle. Later in her track career she set world records in the 100 meter and 200 meter events. She was considered the fastest women on the planet during this time.

It is easy to find reasons to quit or give up on your goals and dreams.

Think of Wilma Rudolph and think of reasons to stick with your dreams.

In other words, everyone has bad days and difficult obstacles to deal with. Many times great athletes, musicians, all kinds of people feel like they are just too tired or too bored to keep working or to keep practicing. This is very normal. Everyone can come up with lots of reasons to quit or give up, but the special people just need to come up with **one good reason** not to quit. One good reason to keep working for your goals and dreams.

Treasure Page
What does your family think?

Sometimes families can be very supportive and really help you with your martial arts training, but some families are less supportive. Regardless, your family its very important and so is what they think.

Here's what to do:

1. Have someone take a photo of you with your family. If some family member helps you with your martial arts training, you may want to have a photo of them helping you.

2. If you do not have a photo, then draw a picture of you and your family. If you don't think you can draw well enough, then make it a fun picture like a cartoon. You may want to label and date the picture.

3. Put the picture or photo below.

4. Now answer the following questions:

* How does your family feel about you doing a martial art?

* Who is your biggest fan and why?

* What was the proudest martial arts moment with your family?

* What was your most embarrassing martial arts moment?

GAME PAGE: Quotes!

What did the author say?

If you don't dream, you may as well be dead.
George Foreman, former heavyweight boxing champ

What do you think (in your own words) George Foreman meant?

_____

_____

_____

_____

How do you think this is important to you in your daily life?

_____

_____

_____

_____

GAME PAGE: Scramble
Martial Arts--Translations

Here are ten martial arts.

aikido * kenpo * * tae kwon do * hapkido

kendo * karate * kung fu * jujutsu * judo * kali

Unscramble the words below and discover what they mean.

taraek _____   empty hand

ungk uf ____ __   great achievement or hard work

stujuuj _____   gentle or flexible art

udoj ____   way of gentleness

lika ____   from kalis, or blade

okidia _____   way of harmony

openko _____   way of the fist

eat wonk od ___ ___ __   way of kicking and punching

kidapho _____   way of spirit/body harmony

denok _____   way of the sword

GAME PAGE: Find the Country of Origin

Draw a line from the martial art to the country of origin located on the map.

<u>Martial Art</u>

karate   Okinawa
kung fu   China
jujutsu   Japan
judo   Japan
kali   Philippine Islands
aikido   Japan
kenpo   China
tae kwon do   Korea
hapkido   Korea
kendo   Japan

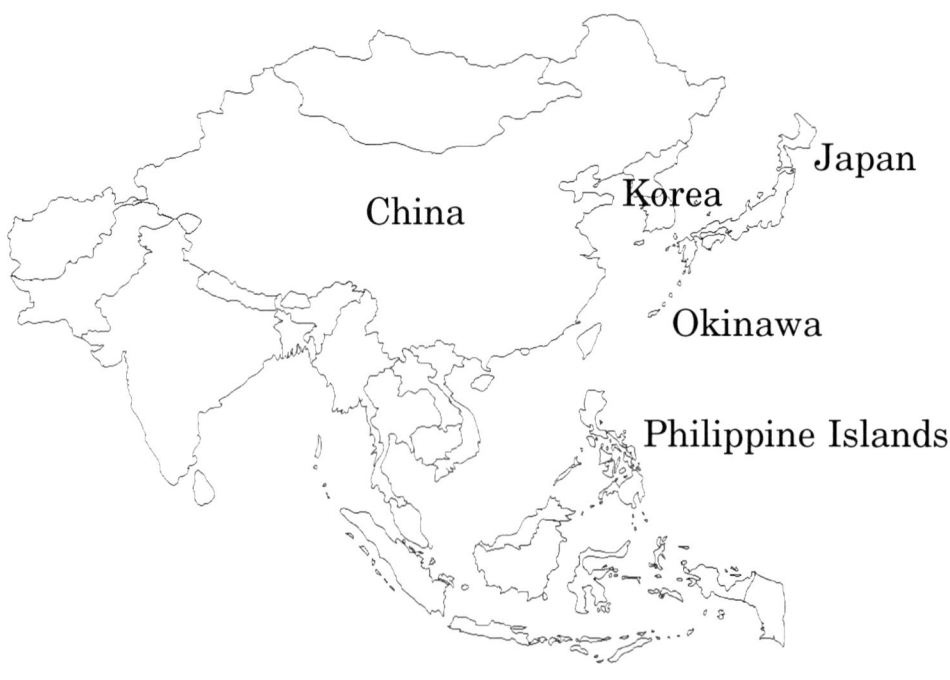

GAME PAGE: Martial Arts Movie Stars

See if you can help unscramble these famous martial artists.

_____ ___   RUBCE EEL

This martial artist was born in San Francisco in 1940. He spent his youth in Hong Kong, and when he returned to the United States, all he had to his name was $100. He began his new life by washing dishes in a Chinese restaurant and starting a kung fu school at a local college. Even though he died over 20 years ago many people consider him the greatest martial arts star ever! Hint: **Enter the Dragon**.

_____ ___   AEIKCJ NAHC

This martial artist--movie star does kung fu/action comedies and he started in movies when he was only seven. He does all of his own stunts many of them are outrageously funny and sometimes death-defying. Hint: **Rumble in the Bronx**.

____ _____   KUCHC SONRRI

This star was one of America's great martial artists even before he got into movies. He is a real fighter & was the undefeated middleweight karate champ in the 1960s. Hint: **Walker, Texas Ranger**.

___-_____ __ ____   ANJE-DULACE NAV EMMAD

This movie star has a thick Belgian accent and has been called "The Muscles from Brussels." He has good looks, a sense of humor, and a great physique. Hint: **Bloodsport**.

GOALS: How dreams come true!

Hard or Long-term goal:

_____

_____ **Day completed:** _____

Short Term Goal	Day Started	Day Completed

GOALS: How dreams come true!

Hard or Long-term goal:

_____

_____ **Day completed:** _____

Short Term Goal	Day Started	Day Completed

GOALS: How dreams come true!

Hard or Long-term goal:

_____

_____ **Day completed:** _____

Short Term Goal	Day Started	Day Completed

GOALS: How dreams come true!

Hard or Long-term goal:

_____

_____ **Day completed:** _____

Short Term Goal	Day Started	Day Completed

GOALS: How dreams come true!

Hard or Long-term goal:

_____

_____ **Day completed:** _____

Short Term Goal	Day Started	Day Completed

GOALS: How dreams come true!

Hard or Long-term goal:

_____

_____ **Day completed:** _____

Short Term Goal	Day Started	Day Completed

GOALS: How dreams come true!

Hard or Long-term goal:

_____

_____ **Day completed:** _____

Short Term Goal	Day Started	Day Completed

GOALS: How dreams come true!

Hard or Long-term goal:

_____

_____ **Day completed:** _____

Short Term Goal	Day Started	Day Completed

GOALS: How dreams come true!

Hard or Long-term goal:

_____

_____ **Day completed:** _____

Short Term Goal	Day Started	Day Completed

Progress Charts
Measuring Your Progress and Growth

There are six important things to keep in mind when you are using your progress charts:

1. What is important to you? Remember this is your book. This is your martial arts training diary. Most importantly, this is your martial arts journey. You can not have someone else decide what you want to do or be! It is very easy to let others tell you what they want, but it is very important for you to decide what you want!

The pages in this chapter are progress charts. You will find that you will not make much progress if you are working on things that are not your goals but goals that belong to others. It is very important to make sure you are deciding on activities that are important to you. You must be very honest with yourself and keep your goals in mind. If you pick something you want to keep in your progress chart section and find that you don't spend much time doing it, and consequently are not making much progress, then maybe there is something more important you should be keeping track of. If you look back at your goals and decide, "I really need to be doing this if I want to accomplish my goal" then knowing how much you want to accomplish your goal will help you reach down inside and find the will power to do the right things.

For example, you may want to stay home on Saturday morning, skip your martial arts class, and watch cartoons, but maybe your goal is to get your brown belt. Well, which would be more fun: one morning of cartoons or getting your brown belt? You decide! Keep in mind when you decide it is **not** with words or what you say but **how you act.** Let your actions do your talking! Let your actions tell what is important to you.

2. Develop Strategies. This is one of the most important things you will ever learn in your entire life! Do you know what developing or planning a strategy means? Well, you have probably seen it hundreds of times, and you probably have done it thousands of times without realizing you were actually doing it.

It is when the hero gets caught by the villain in the movie and things look bad, and I mean very, very bad. At this point, most people would give up but not our hero. He makes a plan! He develops a strategy. He figures a way out of his predicament and how to save the world too!

Make a plan or strategy and keep the results on your progress charts. Sometimes your first strategy will work fine, but many times you will want better results and therefore need to devise a better strategy. By keeping notes in your progress section you will discover your best strategies and be able to use them when you need them in the future.

3. To Be What You Want To Be - Spend Time Doing It! If there is something you want to improve, then spend time working on it. If there is something you want to be one day spend time being it (or work toward being it). Time is kind of like money. If you have a little bit of money, you can buy a candy bar. If you have a lot more money, you could buy a whole candy store. If you really had a whole bunch of money, you could buy the entire candy company, trucks, factories, everything! Basically, it works like this, the more money you have to invest, the bigger and more exciting the items are that you are capable of buying.

Well, time can be a much more valuable investment than money. If you want to be a physician, a great painter, a pro baseball player, a star actor, a musician, a person who can sing a song, or someone who can break three inches of wood with a side kick, no matter how rich you are (even if you are a millionaire or billionaire) you can not do any of these things unless you are willing to invest **time.**

4. There Are Many Different Things to Measure. Everybody is different, so everybody has different things that are important to them. You measure things that are important to you. Even though people measure all kinds of things in their progress charts, I think most things fall in three basic areas: physical things about themselves, doing things, and not doing things.

Physical things might include the following: how tall they are, how much they weigh, waist measurement, size of their arms, dress size, or maybe even how much fat they have (percent of body fat). These are all measurements that are related to their physical bodies. Some people want to get taller, or have bigger muscles, or even have a smaller waist.

Doing things are really activities or actions. You might measure how fast you run a mile, how far you can do splits with your legs, how often you go to your martial arts class, how many boards you can break, how many times you help people, how often you do certain exercises, how high you can kick, how far you can jump, or how often you clean your room. It can be anything your are interested in keeping track of how you are doing. In other words keeping track of your progress.

Not doing things are actions or activities that you are trying to stop or do less often. These are things you measure and you hope the numbers keep getting smaller. You could say these are like bad habits that you want to lessen or get rid of completely. Another way to think of this is think of problems you want to solve.

For example, you might sometimes lose control of your temper at school or in your martial arts class. You might want to keep track of these times and see what helps and what doesn't. Even if you can not figure out ways to fix a problem, by keeping track you will know better what your problem is and this will help you understand it better. That always helps!

It would be impossible to mention everything you might want to put in your progress charts, but hopefully you have already come up with some things that are important to you.

5. Different ways to measure. The first method of measuring that comes to mind is just plain counting. Earlier we said that if you want to be good at something or improve at a particular skill, then you must spend time doing it. So, keeping track of your regular practice is a good idea. You can count how many classes you attend each week or how many times you practice on your own away from class. One time I heard a student ask a grand master how they could improve their side kick. He said, "Kick the bag 10,000 times." At first I thought this was kind of an outrageous answer because I thought how could anyone kick the bag that many times. Then I realized that the only way you could do it is by kicking the bag regularly each week, then weeks add up to months, and months add up to years, and that how you get a great side kick with 10,000 kicks. **Simple counting is a good way to chart your progress.**

The next method is when you use different measuring devices, such as scales, stop watches or timers, tape measures, and so on. The most important thing is to be consistent. Measure things the same way each time. Measure the same way each time so that the changes you see are real changes that reflect your hard work.

The last method is for things that are really hard to measure. For example, let's say you are working on a new form and you want to see how you are doing. Ask a friend, who knows about your martial art, to watch you do your form. Ask them to watch it and then tell them this is what you would call a 5 on a scale from 1 to 10. (You call this a 5 because you want to have room to go up if you improve and have room to go down if you don't.) Now, after you work on your form some more, you can ask that friend to watch it again and see what score they give your form compared to the first time when you had a 5. If you get a 7 then you know your friend thinks it is better. If you get a 3 you know that they think it is not as good.

You can use this scale with jumping kicks, simple moves and easy or difficult techniques, behavior, anything you think is hard to measure. It is fun to mark these scores in your diary. If your friends' names are Wally or Sue you can write in your diary, "Well today I only got a 7 on the Wally scale but I received a 9 1/2 on the Sue scale. It is also fun to keep a scale of your own when you talk to your friends about how hard or easy your workout was when you attend class.

6. Find Advisors: People Who Can Help You. (Probably The Most Important Secret to Success!). This is very important for keeping your progress charts, but it is extremely important for learning about anything that is important to you. The skill that you need to develop is learning to identify those people who are good at helping you and are the type of people you enjoy working with.

Sometimes it is wise to watch how people do things in and outside of class. If you think someone has a great kick, you can just ask them if they wouldn't mind helping you with yours sometime. Another thing to keep in mind is to look at the different belt ranks. Higher belts should know more than lower belts, and often like to help lower belts.

Probably the best place to start when seeking advice about your martial art and your progress charts is your instructor. If it is difficult to have individual time with your head instructor, then you can talk with some of the assistant instructors.

Remember if you want to make progress, then write it down-- Good or Bad!

Grete Waitz

Possibly The Greatest Woman Marathoner ever

Grete Waitz ran marathons, a very long and tiring race of 26.2 miles. She won the New York City Marathon many years in a row. She won races all over the world and held the world record for many years. Here is what she has to say:

> For every finish-line tape a runner breaks - complete with the cheers of the crowd and the clicking of the hundreds of cameras - there are hours of hard and often lonely work that rarely get talked about.

In other words, when you see Grete Waitz or anyone win a race, be wise enough to appreciate the long hours of hard work that must be done before the race even begins. So when you dream of accomplishing some goal that is very important to you, be wise and see the complete picture - the hours of hard work and the moment of glory! It is all good and it is all important.

Treasure Page
What do your friends think?

Sometimes friends can be very supportive and really help you with your martial arts training, but some friends are less supportive. Regardless, your friends are very important and so is what they think.

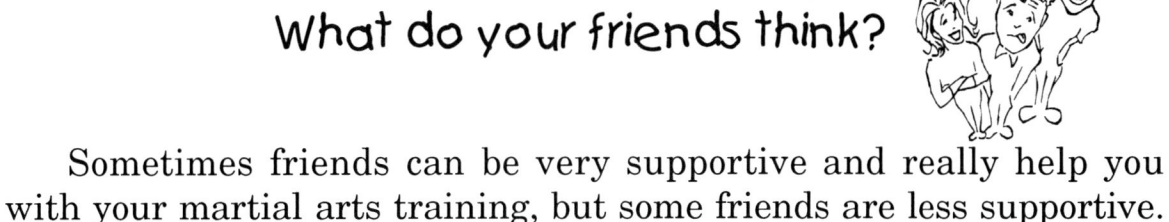

Here's what to do:

1. Have someone take a photo of you with some of your friends. or draw a picture of you and some of your friends. Label and date it.

2. Put the picture or photo on the preceding page.

3. Now answer the following questions:

* What do your friends say about your martial arts training?

* Do you tell many of your friends about your martial art? Why?

* Are any of your friends involved with your martial art?

* Have you made new friends since joining martial arts class?

GAME PAGE:
The Ruler Game - A Reaction Drill

Actions and Reactions. The Ruler Reaction Drill Game is a very simple and fun game, but the most important part of the game is to make you think about your reactions. When you are doing your martial art you may have someone do something to you, for example, it could be a punch, kick or grab. That is an **action**. What you do next is your **reaction**. Developing quick reactions is important in martial arts.

Ruler Reaction Drill Game. This game is played with two players. They can sit down or be standing up. The players must be about an arm's length apart. One player holds a ruler in his/her finger tips. The other player holds their own hand so the thumb and forefinger are in a U shape about two inches apart.

The Object of the Game. One person is the **dropper** and the other person is the **catcher**. The object of the game is for the catcher to catch the ruler as soon as possible. The dropper can hold the ruler as long as they want (up to 30 seconds), but as soon as the catcher sees the ruler move they should snap their fingers together as quickly as possible and catch the ruler. Then the catcher and the dropper should switch.

Scoring. You use the numbers on the ruler to determine how quick your reaction is to the moving ruler. Most rulers have inches and centimeters. You can use either side, but I do think the centimeter side will work better. The dropper should hold the ruler with the highest number at the top and the lowest number hanging down at the bottom. The catcher should keep their fingers at the bottom of the ruler to start. After the drop see what number your fingers stopped the ruler. The lower the number the better the score because the lower the number the quicker or faster your reaction was.

The Martial Arts

```
O O K A L B Z J P R G V I Y A
D X U F G N U K N O Q X O E E
N I L C A J N W E Y X I U B Z
O M E H U C S J D M G N L E F
W L J T Y Y T Y U Y P O H P E
K Z S E A A E K G E D O A Q J
E U X V B R K S T N G N H L V
A I K I D O A I E J P A H O Z
T P N E M D G K S K T C T F Z
```

See if you can find the following MARTIAL ARTS in the WORD-SEARCH above.

- Aikido
- Jujutsu
- Karate
- Kempo
- Kendo
- Kungfu
- Tae Kwon Do

GAME PAGE: Scramble
Martial Arts-Techniques

Here are 13 Martial Arts techniques some common, some uncommon:

* flying kick * lock * hold * knife hand * ridge hand * reverse punch * snap kick * stamping kick * sweep * spear hand * hammer fist * back fist * one-knuckle fist *

Unscramble the words below and discover what these techniques are.

finek dhna _____ ___ (karate chop uses the outside edge of hand)

digre nahd _____ ___ (opposite of knife hand uses inside edge)

reaps adnh _____ ___ (thrusting blow where finger tips are used)

remmah stif _____ ___ (using the fist in hammer like fashion)

kacb sfit ___ ___ (using the back side of the fist)

clok ____ (technique that immobilizes opponents joint)

noe ckuklen tifs ___ _____ ___ (fist where middle joint of index leads)

seeverr chupn _____ ____ (thrown with fist opposite leading leg)

pans ikkc ___ ___ (any kick which is quickly retrieved after use)

pamingts kkic _____ ___ (kick which drives heel downward)

dolh ___ (an immobilizing technique capable of holding a person)

ginfly cikk _____ ___ (kick delivered with both feet off the floor)

epews ___ (an opponents foot is kicked out from under him)

GAME PAGE: Quotes!

What did the author say?

Whether you think you can or think you can't--you are right.
-Henry Ford, American industrialist

What do **you** think (in your own words) Henry Ford meant?

_____

_____

_____

_____

How do **you** think this is important to you in your daily life?

_____

_____

_____

_____

The Martial Arts Training Diary for Kids!

Activity you are Measuring:	
Date	Activity

Activity you are Measuring:	
Date	Activity

Activity you are Measuring:	
Date	Activity

Activity you are Measuring:	
Date	Activity

Activity you are Measuring:	
Date	Activity

Activity you are Measuring:	
Date	Activity

Activity you are Measuring:	
Date	Activity

Activity you are Measuring:	
Date	Activity

The Martial Arts Training Diary for Kids!

Activity you are Measuring:	
Date	**Activity**

Activity you are Measuring:	
Date	**Activity**

Forms
Fighting Imaginary Opponents

Forms (or katas) are extremely important for any type of martial arts training. Some forms have only a few moves and others may have over a hundred moves. These predetermined sequences of moves are the best exercise idea ever! How else can you practice hitting, kicking, punching, and blocking without getting hurt or without hurting someone else? You can practice how you would react if a bad guy was trying to attack you. You can practice reacting instantly and with maximum power. And to top it off, your muscles just get stronger and faster. The more you put into your forms training the more you will improve.

The first challenge in working on your forms is you must learn all the moves of your new form. Your martial arts training diary will help you in two important ways: The first way is for you to keep it nearby when you are in class learning your form from your instructor. Most instructors will think it is a good idea for you to write down the things you are trying to remember. You can even draw pictures or make diagrams. Anything that might help you to remember the moves of your new form (or ways to improve old forms) is worth a try.

The second way your martial arts training diary can help you improve your forms is to keep it nearby when you are practicing your forms at home or away from your regular class. When you are practicing away from class is the time that you will probably have your best questions about your forms. It is very difficult to remember these questions later. So write your questions down during practice and when you get to class, check your training diary to see what you need to ask.

In general, the notes you take in class will tend to be answers or facts, and the notes you take while you are training on your own will tend to be questions.

Sometimes you will hear a student say, "I'm all done I know my form!" Well, sometimes when you finally learn your form you feel like you are finished because you now know all the moves. You can go from start to the end, so you think are finished. Actually, you are not finished or at the end of learning your form, you are actually at the beginning. Now that you have your form (and moves) memorized, you can begin the exciting part--the best part.

Let me explain it in another way. Pretend that learning your form is like building a great car. Now if you worked months or maybe even years to build this exciting car would you just walk away from it when it was done? I don't think so. I bet you would want to get into it and ride it and go on exciting adventures. Your forms training is one of the vehicles you use on your martial arts adventure. Each time you try your form you will think of new ways to improve how you do it. You will think of ways to make your muscles work stronger, new ways to make your techniques more powerful. And sometimes you will just want to take your form and go for a ride or show it off to some friends.

Lastly, remember the more you practice your forms the better your forms will become and as a side benefit, you will become stronger and tougher. Now let's make one point very clear: When I say practice your forms, I am talking about trying your best to be strong and to do the techniques the best you can possibly do them. I am not talking about sloppy practicing or weak practice. If you practice weak, then you get weak. If you practice strong, then you get strong. Practice the best you can because you deserve the best results.

Practice strong and practice smart.

Jackie Robinson
First Black Baseball Player In The Major Leagues

Jackie Robinson was born in Georgia in 1919. His sharecropper father left him when he was only six months old. His mother and his four brothers and sisters were very poor so his mother moved to California in hopes of finding a better life. As Jackie grew he excelled at many sports. He was so good at baseball the owner of the Brooklyn Dodgers, Branch Rickey, decided to have Jackie play on his major league team. Many people made it very difficult for Jackie. Many coaches, fans, and players did not want to see a black man do well. At times Jackie wanted to give up, but he had tremendous courage to stick with it. He not only made the team he also won many awards including Rookie of the Year, and the Most Valuable Player award. Once Jackie was asked how he found so much courage to deal with all the pressure. He said he remembered something an older friend told him when he was young and hanging out with a gang:

He told me that it didn't take guts to follow the crowd, that courage and intelligence lay in being willing to be different.

In other words, if you want to accomplish great things or maybe just those things that are important to you then you must be willing to be different. You must be willing to travel your own path. If "everyone else is doing it" but you don't think it is right, then have the courage to do the right thing.

Treasure Page

Do you think you will get a black belt?

Here's what to do:

1. List five reasons why you think you will get a black belt.

2. List five reasons why you don't think you will get a black belt?

Martial Arts Translations

Across

2. Teacher, Japan
5. Training Room Japan
7. Padded Post or Board
9. Wooden Pole

Down

1. Signifies Rank
2. Teacher, Korean
3. Two Wooded Batons
4. Respectful Bending
5. Training Room Karean
6. Elementary Technique
7. Teacher, Chinese

GAME PAGE: Quotes!

What did the author say?

When the one Great Scorer comes to write against your name, He marks not that you won or lost, but how you played the game. *-Grantland Rice*

What do **you** think (in your own words) Grantland Rice meant?

_____

_____

_____

How do **you** think this is important to you in your daily life?

_____

_____

_____

_____

GAME PAGE: Matching
Common Techniques and Definitions

Draw a line from the technique to the correct definition.

Techniques	Definitions
spear hand	karate chop uses the outside edge of hand
snap kick	opposite of knife hand uses inside edge
lock	thrusting blow where finger tips are used
ridge hand	using the bottom of the fist in a downward or sideways motion--hammer like fashion
knife hand	using the back side of the fist
back fist	technique that immobilizes opponents joint
flying kick	fist with middle joint of index (or middle finger) leads others
hold	thrown with opposite fist to leading leg
hammer fist	kick which is quickly retrieved after use
stamping kick	kick which drives heel downward
sweep	an immobilizing technique for holding a person without necessarily hurting him
reverse punch	any kick which is delivered when both feet are off the floor
one knuckle fist	an opponents foot is kicked out from under him and he loses his balance

FORMS: Fighting Imaginary Opponents

Form:　　　　**Date:**　　　　**Instructor:**

Comments:

Form:　　　　**Date:**　　　　**Instructor:**

Comments:

Form:　　　　**Date:**　　　　**Instructor:**

Comments:

FORMS: Fighting Imaginary Opponents

Form:	**Date:**	**Instructor:**
Comments:		

Form:	**Date:**	**Instructor:**
Comments:		

Form:	**Date:**	**Instructor:**
Comments:		

FORMS: Fighting Imaginary Opponents

Form:	Date:	Instructor:
Comments:		

Form:	Date:	Instructor:
Comments:		

Form:	Date:	Instructor:
Comments:		

FORMS: Fighting Imaginary Opponents

Form:	Date:	Instructor:
Comments:		

Form:	Date:	Instructor:
Comments:		

Form:	Date:	Instructor:
Comments:		

Opponent: **Belt:** **Date:**

Observations:

Advice:

Opponent: **Belt:** **Date:**

Observations:

Advice:

Opponent: **Belt:** **Date:**

Observations:

Advice:

| **Opponent:** | **Belt:** | **Date:** |

Observations:

Advice:

| **Opponent:** | **Belt:** | **Date:** |

Observations:

Advice:

| **Opponent:** | **Belt:** | **Date:** |

Observations:

Advice:

Sparring
Putting It All Together

When people talk about sparring (or fighting) in their martial arts class, they could be talking about one of many different activities that fall under the same label. For example, your friend could be taking Tae Kwon Do and you could be studying Tae Kwon Do. You may need to buy equipment (headgear, pads, and a mouth piece), he may only need a uniform. One martial arts group may use light contact in their training where they lightly touch their opponents in sparring. Some groups have full contact and some have no contact at all! There are many differences, but there are many important things which are the same for all martial artists.

The following are some areas you may want to think about when you write down your thoughts in the sparring section of your martial arts training diary. It will be exciting to see how you change and grow during your martial arts journey:

1. Sparring should be fun. By fun, I do not mean silly fun but rather serious fun. The kind of fun I am talking about is where you work very hard and feel good about your improvement, your skill level in sparring, and about yourself overall. If you feel there are any problems when you are doing your sparring, then work on those specific areas.

For example, if you are afraid of getting hurt, then figure out a way to change your technique or your style so you do not get hurt.

Maybe you are doing things correctly and someone in the class is doing something wrong resulting in your being injured. If so then it might be time to sit down with a senior belt or an instructor and ask them for advice.

If it bothers you to lose when you are sparring (I mean you get really upset), then talk to someone about that and see if you can adjust your attitude so you can appreciate the positive aspects. For example, if you are sparring people who are better skilled than you most of the time, then you are probably being challenged and forced to do your best. It is guaranteed that you are improving more than a person who is constantly sparring people they can easily defeat and consequently these opponents represent no challenge at all. Remember: **No challenge no growth!**

In general, the most important thing to remember is the only way you will really improve is if you work out regularly and if you continue your martial arts training for a long time. If sparring is not enjoyable you will find it extremely difficult to stick with it.

2. You should feel safe. Your martial arts class and sparring should be a place where you feel reasonably safe. You go to class to learn and grow. No one wants you to be hurt or injured. If you or your parents feel your class is unsafe then maybe it is time to leave and find one where you feel more comfortable. Again, if you do not feel safe you will find it difficult to make yourself go to class. If you don't go to class then you can not grow and improve.

3. How are you doing? It is very difficult for anyone at any age to determine how well or how poorly they are doing. However, when you write in your training diary you can keep track of your sparring progress in different ways. You can write down how you feel you are doing in your sparring. You can keep track of the number of points you scored or how many matches you won. How many kicks or punches you get in or how many you avoid or block. You can keep a record of the comments your instructors make or comments made by others (fellow students, senior students, or family members).

4. What are your opponents doing against you? In the sparring section of your martial arts training diary, you might want to keep notes on some of your special opponents. You might have one opponent you go against regularly in your class. This person might be about the same level as you are but whenever you spar, he or she always seems to do a technique that surprises you. For example, in the middle of a match when things are very hectic, his or her favorite thing to do might be to try a high roundhouse kick on you. Or another opponent might like to start a match with a combination of a front kick followed by an punch. By keeping track of these tendencies you will start to develop strategies for stopping your opponents' favorite attacks and develop plans for taking advantage of them.

5. What are you doing against your opponents? You might find it useful to keep track of two things: What works and what doesn't! It is very good to keep track of those techniques or attacks that work for you. Some people do something that I think is very wise. When they find something that is very successful they kind of put it away. They know that particular technique works so they put it away and take out something that they want to develop and make better. For example, if you find that most of the time you try a double side kick on someone it usually gets in for a point, then you might want to put it aside and work on your back spinning side kick.

Now maybe every time you try a roundhouse kick with your back leg your opponents seem ready and they almost always block it, then you might want to experiment with a new twist. You might want to try sneaking in a roundhouse kick with your front leg to catch them off guard. Or you might want to try doing a few side kicks in a row to set up your roundhouse kick. The most important thing is to learn how to analyze (think about) your sparring.

6. What do you like best about sparring? What do you like least about sparring? It is always fun to keep notes on these types of thoughts because it is fascinating to see how much they will change. You will find new things that might make you feel uncomfortable and you will look back at your sparring notes and find old solutions from earlier concerns that will work with your new concerns. More importantly, as you see how much your comments change over the weeks and years you will see how much you have grown as a martial artist during your martial arts journey

7. Who can you go to for help with your sparring? You can go to your main or head instructor, assistant instructors, senior students, higher belts, and others. You will find some people make you feel very comfortable about asking questions and getting help and other people make you feel funny. You also might find that some people make you feel great but their advice does not seem to work. This is an important skill to learn. You want to find people who can help you solve problems when you can not solve them yourself.

One last comment about sparring. My instructor once said, "You spar as you are and you are as you spar." This means if in your everyday life you find you are afraid to try new things or new adventures, then you will probably be the same in your sparring and will be afraid to try new things. Also, if you are the kind of person who bulls ahead in sparring and does not think about the consequences, then you are probably the same way when you have to deal with things in your regular day to day activities.

So the exciting part is if there are things about yourself that you would like to change, then your martial arts sparring maybe be the best place to start making those changes. If you want to try more new things in your life then try new things in your sparring. If you want to worry less about things in general, then try to approach your sparring with an attitude where you are just going to have fun and enjoy it.

James J. Corbett
World Heavyweight Bare Knuckle Champion Boxer

James J. Corbett was a boxer back in the old days before they used gloves. The fighters would "toe the line" at the start of each round. If the fighter got knocked down or was thrown down, the round would be over, they would get a minute rest, and have to toe the line for the next round. Some of these fights would last over 100 rounds and take hours! Today's longest boxing matches last only 15 rounds. Needless to say, these men were extremely tough, and James J. Corbett was the best of them all! Here's what he had to say:

You become a champ by fighting one more round. When things are tough, you fight one more round.

In other words, if you really want something in life like making all A's, making the team, being first string, making first chair in the orchestra, getting a college scholarship, getting a job, or getting a black belt--anything, just remember don't give up. James J. Corbett did **not** say fight the best round of your life or the best round in world record history, he just said keep trying--don't give up. So when things get tough and you feel like giving up on your **dreams**, think of what the best and toughest bare knuckle fighter in history used to tell himself: **Just fight one more round.**

Treasure Page
The TOURNAMENT!

So you have decided to enter a tournament. No matter how old you are or what your belt rank is, entering a tournament is a very big deal! Everybody gets nervous and excited, but people always have fun and most people are very glad they did it regardless of the results. Good luck in yours!

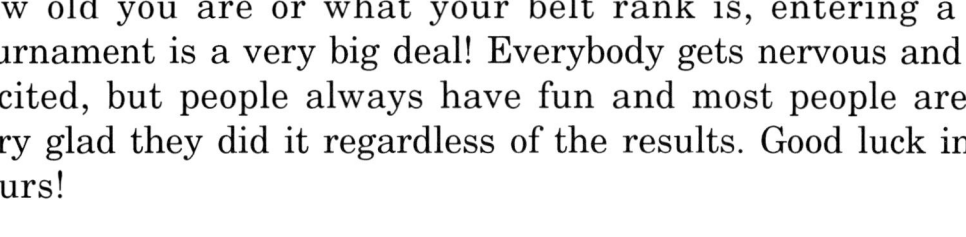

Here's what to do:

Get a friend or family member to interview you just like they do on television. They can use a video camera or just a cassette tape recorder. Here are some suggested before and after questions. Feel free to add any of your own because these are just some starter questions:

BEFORE:

* Why did you decide to enter this tournament?
* What are you most worried about?
* What do you feel most confident about?
* What is your plan for today?
* How good do you think the other people will be?

AFTER:

* How do you feel?
* What was the best part of the tournament?
* What was the worst part?

GAME PAGE: Quotes!

What did the author say?

Desire is the most important factor in the success of any athlete.　　　　　　　　*-Willie Shoemaker, record setting jockey*

What do **you** think (in your own words) Willie Shoemaker meant?

_____

_____

_____

_____

How do **you** think this is important to you in your daily life?

_____

_____

_____

_____

GAME PAGE: Boxes

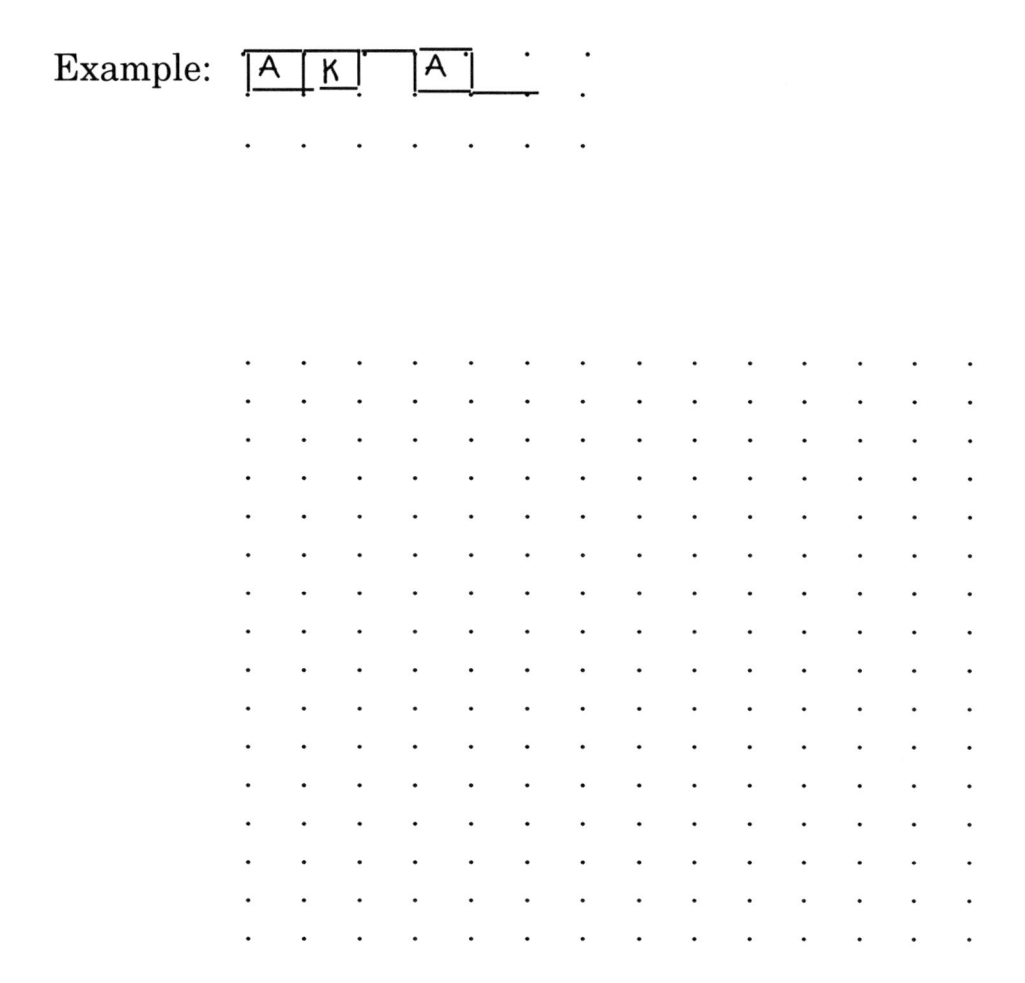

Example: | A | K | A |

This is a game that is played with two or more players. Using the dotted pattern above, the players connect one dot to one of the closest dots. The object of the game is to get the fourth line that competes the box. If you get the fourth side, then it is your box and you put your initial in the box and you get to go again. The player with the most boxes wins.

Games like this make you think of different strategies, and they make you consider how you think your opponents may act. Sometimes you may have to guess or anticipate what your opponents next move might be. All of these skills relate to your martial arts class and your martial arts class can enhance everything you do.

GAME PAGE:
Martial Arts Balloon Game

The Martial Arts Balloon Game is played with one or more players. The game is a little easier if the balloon is shaped like a ball (other shapes are more difficult but also fun).

Normal Game. Here is how the game is played. The players get together and one player throws the balloon into the air. Then the players try to keep the balloon in the air as long as possible without it touching the ground. Every time someone hits the balloon to keep it up in the air the players count the hit.

Sounds pretty easy--well here's the catch.

Martial Arts Game. When you play the martial arts way you are only allowed to hit the balloon with martial arts techniques. You can punch, block, use feet, elbows, knees, head, anything that is a martial arts move.

Training Diary Note. If you play this game often, it is a good idea to keep the record (most hits that day) and the players' names written in your training diary.

GAME PAGE: Matching

Martial Arts: Terms and Definitions

Draw a line from the term to the correct definition.

TERMS	DEFINITIONS
dojang	elementary techniques of a martial art
makiwara	fabric worn around the waist--signifies rank
sabom	bending of body to shows respect
belt	rank of black belts
sifu	place of training (Korean)
sensei	place of training (Japanese)
staff	padded training post or board (Japanese)
bow	two wooded batons linked by a chain or chord
dojo	teacher (Korean)
basics	teacher (Japanese)
nunchaku	teacher (Chinese)
dan	wooden pole about six feet long

| **Opponent:** | **Belt:** | **Date:** |

Observations:

Advice:

| **Opponent:** | **Belt:** | **Date:** |

Observations:

Advice:

| **Opponent:** | **Belt:** | **Date:** |

Observations:

Advice:

The Martial Arts Training Diary for Kids!

| **Opponent:** | **Belt:** | **Date:** |

Observations:

Advice:

| **Opponent:** | **Belt:** | **Date:** |

Observations:

Advice:

| **Opponent:** | **Belt:** | **Date:** |

Observations:

Advice:

| **Opponent:** | **Belt:** | **Date:** |

Observations:

Advice:

| **Opponent:** | **Belt:** | **Date:** |

Observations:

Advice:

| **Opponent:** | **Belt:** | **Date:** |

Observations:

Advice:

Opponent:	**Belt:**	**Date:**
Observations:		
Advice:		

Opponent:	**Belt:**	**Date:**
Observations:		
Advice:		

Opponent:	**Belt:**	**Date:**
Observations:		
Advice:		

Opponent:	Belt:	Date:
Observations:		
Advice:		

Opponent:	Belt:	Date:
Observations:		
Advice:		

Opponent:	Belt:	Date:
Observations:		
Advice:		

| **Opponent:** | **Belt:** | **Date:** |

Observations:

Advice:

| **Opponent:** | **Belt:** | **Date:** |

Observations:

Advice:

| **Opponent:** | **Belt:** | **Date:** |

Observations:

Advice:

| **Opponent:** | **Belt:** | **Date:** |

Observations:

Advice:

| **Opponent:** | **Belt:** | **Date:** |

Observations:

Advice:

| **Opponent:** | **Belt:** | **Date:** |

Observations:

Advice:

Reflections
So What Do You Think?

When you talk things over with your friends or family, and when you have class discussions in school, it is a good way to learn and get smarter. Also, it makes you feel much better when you are worried or upset about something if you can talk it over with someone. When something really good happens to you most people go running to find someone to tell. This is because thinking about things is good, and thinking through things can help solve problems and make good times extra special.

In this chapter what you think and what you feel are the two most important things. In this chapter it is impossible to make a mistake. You are the boss and you decide what is important and what's not. If you are a brand new student just starting your martial arts journey or an experienced black belt it does not matter because you are already an expert on how you think and feel. The challenge for you in this chapter will be getting these thoughts down on paper.

Even though you are the expert about yourself and what is important to you, here are a few coaching points to help you make your reflections section the best it can be:

1. When in doubt write it down! In the 30 or more years I have been involved with people keeping sports training diaries or any kind of diary, I have never once heard a person say they wrote too much in their diary. Most people wish they had written more. When you get older and you look back at you diary, each little comment will seem like the best sweetest piece of candy you ever had and you will want to read more, but unfortunately you cannot ride down to the neighborhood candy store and get another box. The thoughts, ideas, and feelings you write in your martial arts training diary are precious now and will only increase in value over the years.

2. Plan time to write. Set up a specific time on a regular basis to write. Let's say you write every weekend or right after your martial arts class or maybe every evening before you go to bed. You must decide what is best for you. Also, as time goes on you will probably come up with better ways to do it.

3. Write down the BIG things. If you know a belt test or a tournament is coming up soon, write down your thoughts before the big day, and write down you reactions after the big day. This is very important because you will learn how you handle these exciting but very intense situations. For example, a friend of mine gets really nervous days before a tournament but on the day of the tournament when she walks into the gym where the tournament is being held, she feels totally relaxed and ready to go into action. So by keeping her training diary, she has learned to remind herself that it is OK when she feels nervous before the big day because she knows she will be fine when she walks into the gym.

4. Write down the Good, the Bad, the Ugly - EVERYTHING! Some people feel like you should only write down good things in your diary. Well, I disagree! Did you ever watch a TV show or a movie where only good things happen? If you did, it was probably very boring. Very often the bad or ugly days can be great sources of inspiration. For example, the first time we tried to break boards in my martial arts class everyone was able to do it except me! I was especially embarrassed because I was the biggest one in the class and everyone thought it was going to be really easy for me. Then when I thought I could not be any more embarrassed, I decided to try one more time and I kicked the metal board holder and hurt my foot.

Needless to say, it was a really bad day. When I went home and started to write about it in my martial arts training diary, I was alone in my room, but I was so embarrassed that I kept looking around. I think I was worried someone would see me and find out how bad my day was. However, soon I forgot all about that bad ugly day.

Then one day, years later, I broke eight boards and six concrete blocks at a martial arts demonstration. I felt pretty good about my combination break and decided to record it in my training diary. As I was flipping through the pages to get to the next blank page, I noticed my notes about that bad day when I couldn't even break one board. Reading my notes made me remember that day and how bad I felt. Then it hit me like a big icy wave how much I had improved since then, and I felt WONDERFUL! You also will have bad ugly days and they too will turn into wonderful days. Write them both down.

When in doubt--write it down!

Cori Carson

One of the country's best Basketball players Division III Women

When this Marymount University basketball player was told that she needed a liver transplant, she could not believe it. When the doctors said she only had two hours left to live, she received a liver transplant.

Well, guess what happened to her exactly one year (to the hour) later? She scored 29 points in 19 minutes in Marymount University's season-opening win. Here's what she has to say:

I used to think about the future. Now I try to live each day to the fullest.

In other words, everyone needs to appreciate what a wonderful gift each and every day is and we should try to make the most of it. The secret to big and exciting accomplishments, having a great career, or for that matter, a wonderful life, is doing things one precious day at a time.

Treasure Page
The BELT TEST!

Congratulations, your instructor has just informed you that you are ready for your next belt test! They must think that you are really improving and getting better to pay you such a compliment!

Here's what to do:

Get a friend or family member to interview you just like they do on television. They can use a video camera or just a plan cassette tape recorder. Here are some suggested before and after questions. Feel free to add any of your own because these are just some starter questions:

BEFORE

* How are you feeling?
* Are you worried about anything?
* What do you feel the most confident about?
* How do you think you are going to do?

AFTER

* How do you feel?
* What was the hardest part?
* What part seemed the easiest?
* What would you do differently, if anything, next time?

REFLECTIONS: So What Do You Think?

Date:_____ Topic:_____

_____

_____

_____

_____

Date:_____ Topic:_____

_____

_____

_____

_____

Date:_____ Topic:_____

_____

_____

_____

_____

REFLECTIONS: So What Do You Think?

Date:_____ Topic:_____

_____

_____

_____

Date:_____ Topic:_____

_____

_____

_____

Date:_____ Topic:_____

_____

_____

_____

REFLECTIONS: So What Do You Think?

Date:_____Topic:_____

_____

_____

_____

Date:_____Topic:_____

_____

_____

_____

Date:_____Topic:_____

_____

_____

_____

GAME PAGE:
Tick Tac Toe...And More

Sometimes you can take a fairly simple game and make it more challenging. When you do this you develop many more strategies and become better at solving problems.

For example you can play tick tac toe the normal way. One player is X and the other player is O. You take turns filling in the empty boxes until one player has three in a straight line either up and down, side ways, or diagonally (/).

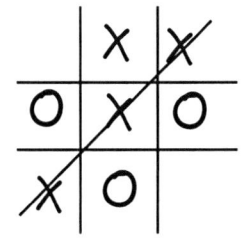

But then if you want a real challenge you can play five, ten, or more games at the same time. This will seem confusing at first but you will be able to handle it.

Another challenge given ... another challenge accepted!

GAME PAGE: Quotes!

What did the author say?

Success doesn't come to you...you go to it.   *-Marva Collins*

What do **you** think (in your own words) Marva Collins meant?

_____

_____

_____

_____

How do **you** think this is important to you in your daily life?

_____

_____

_____

REFLECTIONS: So What Do You Think?

Date:_____ Topic:_____

_____

_____

_____

Date:_____ Topic:_____

_____

_____

_____

Date:_____ Topic:_____

_____

_____

_____

Important Stuff I'd Better Remember!

As you get older and involved with more things, you will find that it becomes more difficult to keep everything straight. You really cannot remember everything you are supposed to do or everything you might need. Well, what is the solution? Just write it down. Instead of trying to have a perfect memory, just write down what you need to know. This way you do not need to remember 10, 20, or 100 things. You just need to remember one thing:

If it is important, then write it down!

This chapter will give you a place to keep all of your important information. Anything you think is important goes in this section. Also, anything that you want to put into your martial arts training diary that does not seem to fit in any of the other sections of this book is welcome in this section. Here are a few examples of items other students have put in this section:

* Important dates: belt tests, special classes or camps, friends' birthdays, holidays, vacation dates, and so on.
* Phone numbers: classmates, friends, instructors.
* Order of belts: cost of belt tests, time requirements.
* Names of favorite martial arts books.
* Names of favorite martial arts movies/videos.
* List of classmates, names of instructors.
* Cost: monthly dues, uniforms, t-shirts, badges, jackets.

NOTES
Important Stuff I'd Better Remember!

NOTES
Important Stuff I'd Better Remember!

NOTES
Important Stuff I'd Better Remember!

NOTES
Important Stuff I'd Better Remember!

Parents' Guide

There have been many studies done, at every educational level, that indicate that students involved with athletics consistently out perform their peers in the classroom. The study and practice of a martial art is without doubt more demanding than many sports in areas such as self discipline, regular practice, and respect for self and others. Also, the amount of success achieved by doing a particular martial art is the sole responsibility of the martial arts practitioner. No one can do it for them. In other words, having your child involved with a martial arts program is an excellent idea, but even the best parents cannot earn a belt for their child. The child is the only one who can do it--and that's good news!

As your child embarks on a wonderful martial arts journey, you realize you can't do it for them and you can't make them do it, but you can be an excellent source of support and encouragement. Here are a few helpful parent coaching points:

* **Be proud of you child's martial arts studies.** Let your child know how proud you are and let your child hear you tell others of your pride. It is difficult for people at any age to attempt to learn something new and different. Also, any individual who is willing to put forth time, effort, and energy in order to improve themselves deserves our respect. This is especially important for a child.

* **Celebrate the big moments.** When your child has made progress (a new belt or rank, entered a tournament, attended a camp, whatever), do something special to demonstrate your excitement for this special accomplishment. Let your child choose a special meal or have family members come around for dessert or plan a special photograph.

* Finally the three most important things to do if you want to help your child with their martial art: 1) Get them to class, 2) Get them to class, and 3) **Get them to class regularly.**

By helping your child capture their experiences in **The Martial Arts Training Diary--FOR KIDS!** you will be helping them in innumerable ways. You will be helping them learn about the martial art of their choice, but more importantly, you will be teaching them how to set goals and how to intelligently pursue those goals. This is a life-long skill which your child will be able to use with any future endeavor. Lastly, your child will learn about themselves and will have a personal record of this journey which they will treasure for a lifetime. Here are some parent coaching points on how to help your child use and maintain their martial arts training diary:

* **Read your child's diary to them.** This will vary at different levels, but all children will benefit from the attention. If your child is very young or a weak reader, then read as much as they need. This pertains to your reading the text of the book and also the child's diary entries. If your child is a nonreader and you read the training diary to them, then ask them questions about their martial arts training and write their responses down in their diary. Make an effort to make them feel empowered. Your role is to just get their thoughts down on paper. Their comments may be serious, silly, or confusing, but I guarantee they will always be interesting and this process will be an absolute delight for you and your child. As a parent, you will create a treasure for yourself and a book that will undoubtedly become your child's favorite book to be read over and over again. Imagine being so young and having a book full of your own personal comments that can be read by anyone they give permission. This gives your child motivation to become a reader.

* **Be prepared to write for them--some.** The key is to get the child to begin a process of thought and discussion. It may be useful at times for the parent or friend to help get the child's responses down in the diary. If your child's ideas and comments are really flying or maybe the child is not feeling very well and they are getting frustrated trying to write things down, it is acceptable for the child to get some help.

* **Learn how to "prime the pump."** Just as a hand pump may need some water to prime it and get things started so the water begins to flow, the same is true about people with regard to thinking, discussing, and writing. For example, when your child has spent 7 or 8 hours away from you at school and you ask what happened at school today and they respond, "Oh, nothing." You know that pump is dry and needs priming. So, you can ask a few priming questions. How did the math test go? What happened at recess? Did anything happen to Sally? Did anything funny happen today? The same is true with your child's martial arts class and the more you try priming, the better you will become. Open ended questions that you have no idea of the answers are usually the most fun and interesting, regardless of the age of your child.

* **Remember, there is no wrong way to keep a diary.** Every decision you make as a parent regarding your child's efforts in keeping his or her martial arts training diary should be directed toward maintaining the process. The most important thing is to keep doing it.

Here are a few examples of the different skills your child will be developing by keeping a martial arts training diary:
* goal and value clarification
* writing and reading for a purpose
* thinking, problem solving
* learn to "stick with" things and see them through
* the concept that hard work helps one improve
* creativity
* learn to assess one's weaknesses and strengths
* learn to assess others' skills
* note taking skills
* self expression

Lastly, your child will develop skills where they will learn how to work hard and smart. Most people believe that you only attain success when you feel you deserve it, and the only way you feel that you deserve it is if you work hard for it! One of the most valuable gifts you can give your child is to help them learn that if they want something or they want to be something, it's there if they are willing to work for it.

Answer Key

Page 55:

Martial Arts Translations

				B					
S	E	N	S	E	I				
A		U		L					
B		N		T				B	
O		C			D	O	J	O	
M		H			O			W	
		A		B	J				
M	A	K	I	W	A	R	A		
		U		S					
				I			S		
				C			I		
				S	T	A	F	F	
							U		

:

Answer Key

Page 27: Scramble

karate:empty hand, kung fu:great achievement or hard work
jujutsu:gentle or flexible art, judo:way of gentleness
kali:from kalis, or blade, aikido:way of harmony
kenpo:way of the fist, tae kwon do:way of kicking and punching
hapkido:way of spirit/body harmony, kendo:way of the sword

Page 29: Movie Stars

Bruce Lee
Jackie Chan
Chuck Norris
Jean-Claude Van Damme

Page 45: Word Search

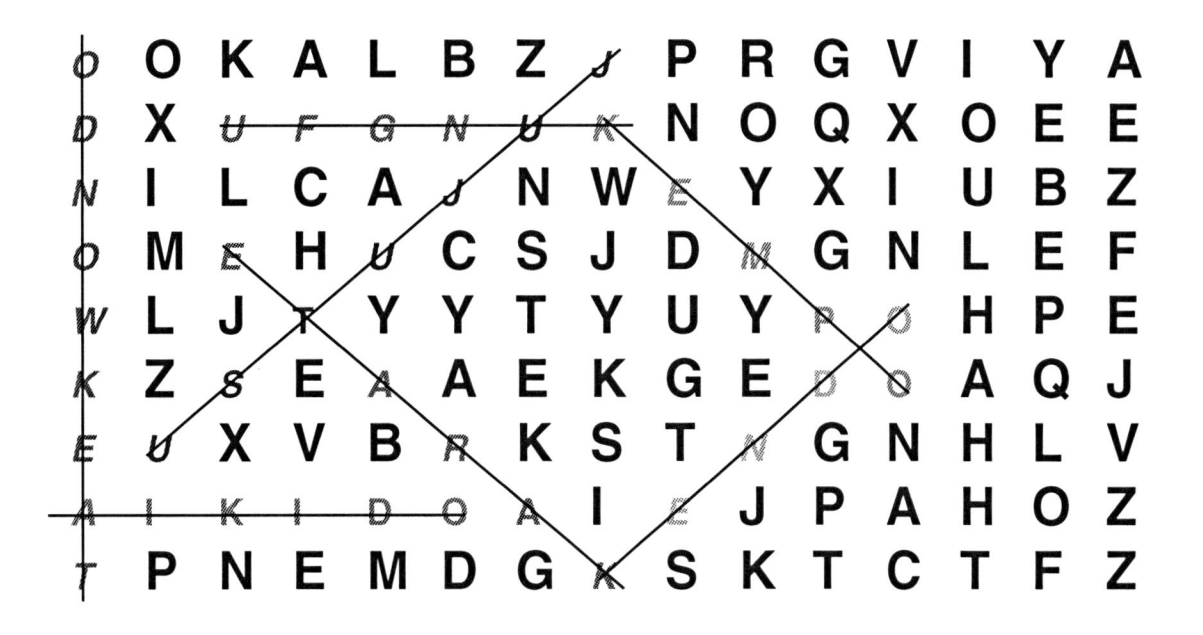

O	K	A	L	B	Z	J	P	R	G	V	I	Y	A
D	X	U	F	G	N	U	K	N	O	Q	X	O	E	E
N	I	L	C	A	J	N	W	E	Y	X	I	U	B	Z
O	M	E	H	U	C	S	J	D	M	G	N	L	E	F
W	L	J	T	Y	Y	T	Y	U	Y	P	O	H	P	E
K	Z	S	E	A	A	E	K	G	E	D	O	A	Q	J
E	U	X	V	B	R	K	S	T	N	O	G	N	H	L	V
A	I	K	I	D	O	A	I	J	P	A	H	O	Z
T	P	N	E	M	D	G	K	S	K	T	C	T	F	Z

105

Answer Key

Page 46 and 57: Answers to Common Techniques

knife hand:	karate chop uses the outside edge of hand
ridge hand:	opposite of knife hand uses inside edge
spear hand:	thrusting blow where finger tips are used
hammer fist:	using the bottom of the fist in a downward or sideways motion
back fist:	using the back side of the fist
lock:	technique that immobilizes opponents joint
one knuckle fist:	fist with middle joint of index leads others
reverse punch:	thrown with opposite fist to leading leg
snap kick:	kick which is quickly retrieved after use
stamping kick:	kick which drives heel downward
hold:	an immobilizing technique capable of holding a person . . .
flying kick:	any kick which is delivered when both feet. . .
sweep:	an opponents foot is kicked out from under him and he loses his balance

Page 71: Answers to Matching

basics:	elementary techniques of a martial art
belt:	fabric worn around the waist--signifies rank
bow:	bending of body which shows respect for oneself and others
dan:	rank of black belts
dojang:	place of training (Korean)
dojo:	place of training (Japanese)
makiwara:	(Japanese) padded training post or board
nunchaku:	two wooded batons linked by a chain or chord
sabom:	teacher (Korean)
sensei:	teacher (Japanese)
sifu:	teacher (Chinese)
staff:	wooden pole about six feet long

Also Available from Turtle Press:

Martial Arts After 40
Warrior Speed
The Martial Arts Training Diary
The Martial Arts Training Diary for Kids
Teaching: The Way of the Master
Combat Strategy
The Art of Harmony
A Guide to Rape Awareness and Prevention
Total MindBody Training
1,001 Ways to Motivate Yourself and Others
Ultimate Fitness through Martial Arts
Weight Training for Martial Artists
Launching a Martial Arts School
Advanced Teaching Report
Hosting a Martial Art Tournament
100 Low Cost Marketing Ideas for the Martial Arts School
A Part of the Ribbon: A Time Travel Adventure
Herding the Ox
Neng Da: Super Punches
250 Ways to Make Classes Fun & Exciting
Martial Arts and the Law
Taekwondo Kyorugi: Olympic Style Sparring
Martial Arts for Women
Parents' Guide to Martial Arts
Strike Like Lightning: Meditations on Nature
Everyday Warriors

For more information:
Turtle Press
PO Box 290206
Wethersfield CT 06129-206
1-800-77-TURTL
e-mail: sales@turtlepress.com

http://www.turtlepress.com